HELEN HALLER
ELEMENTARY LIBRARY
350 Fir Street
Sequim, WA 98382

BEGINNING TO END

Milk to Ice Cream

by Elizabeth Neuenfeldt

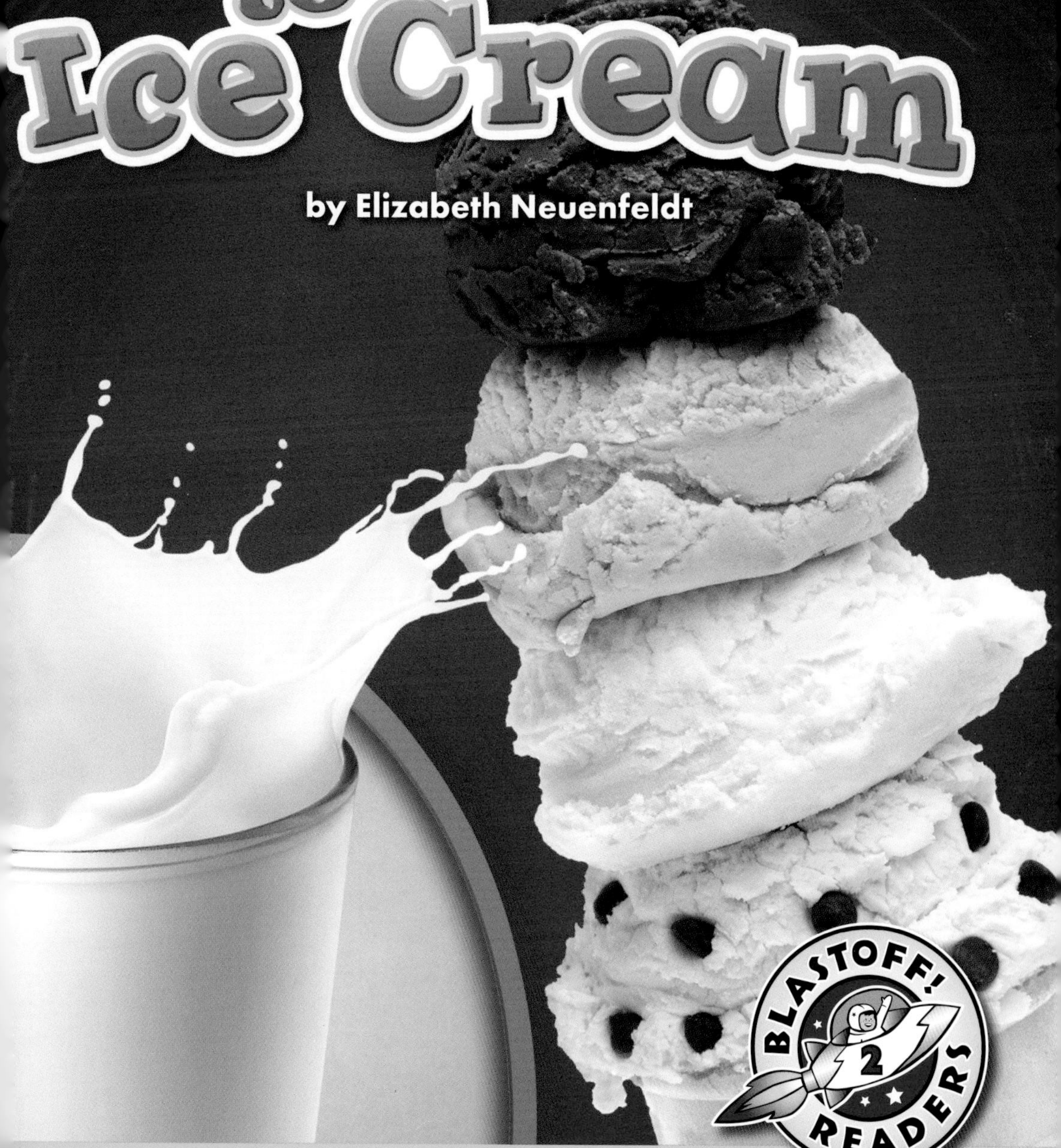

BLASTOFF! READERS 2

BELLWETHER MEDIA • MINNEAPOLIS, MN

Blastoff! Readers are carefully developed by literacy experts to build reading stamina and move students toward fluency by combining standards-based content with developmentally appropriate text.

Level 1 provides the most support through repetition of high-frequency words, light text, predictable sentence patterns, and strong visual support.

Level 2 offers early readers a bit more challenge through varied sentences, increased text load, and text-supportive special features.

Level 3 advances early-fluent readers toward fluency through increased text load, less reliance on photos, advancing concepts, longer sentences, and more complex special features.

★ **Blastoff! Universe**

Reading Level

Grade K

Grades 1–3

Grade 4

This edition first published in 2021 by Bellwether Media, Inc.

No part of this publication may be reproduced in whole or in part without written permission of the publisher. For information regarding permission, write to Bellwether Media, Inc., Attention: Permissions Department, 6012 Blue Circle Drive, Minnetonka, MN 55343.

Library of Congress Cataloging-in-Publication Data

Names: Neuenfeldt, Elizabeth, author.
Title: Milk to ice cream / Elizabeth Neuenfeldt.
Description: Minneapolis, MN : Bellwether Media, Inc., 2021. | Series: Beginning to end | Includes bibliographical references and index. | Audience: Ages 5-8 | Audience: Grades K-1 | Summary: "Relevant images match informative text in this introduction to how milk becomes ice cream. Intended for students in kindergarten through third grade"–Provided by publisher.
Identifiers: LCCN 2020039237 (print) | LCCN 2020039238 (ebook) | ISBN 9781644874226 (library binding) | ISBN 9781648342448 (paperback) | ISBN 9781648340994 (ebook)
Subjects: LCSH: Ice cream, ices, etc.–Juvenile literature. | Dairy products–Juvenile literature.
Classification: LCC TX795 .N48 2021 (print) | LCC TX795 (ebook) | DDC 641.86/2–dc23
LC record available at https://lccn.loc.gov/2020039237
LC ebook record available at https://lccn.loc.gov/2020039238

Text copyright © 2021 by Bellwether Media, Inc. BLASTOFF! READERS and associated logos are trademarks and/or registered trademarks of Bellwether Media, Inc.

Editor: Rebecca Sabelko   Designer: Laura Sowers

Printed in the United States of America, North Mankato, MN.

Table of Contents

A Frozen Treat	4
To the Factory!	6
Mixed and Frozen	10
Ready to Eat!	20
Glossary	22
To Learn More	23
Index	24

A Frozen Treat

How is ice cream made?
It all begins with milk!

Who Eats the Most Ice Cream?

The average New Zealander eats more than 7 gallons (28 liters) of ice cream each year!

Milk comes from cows on dairy farms. A special **process** turns milk into ice cream.

To the Factory!

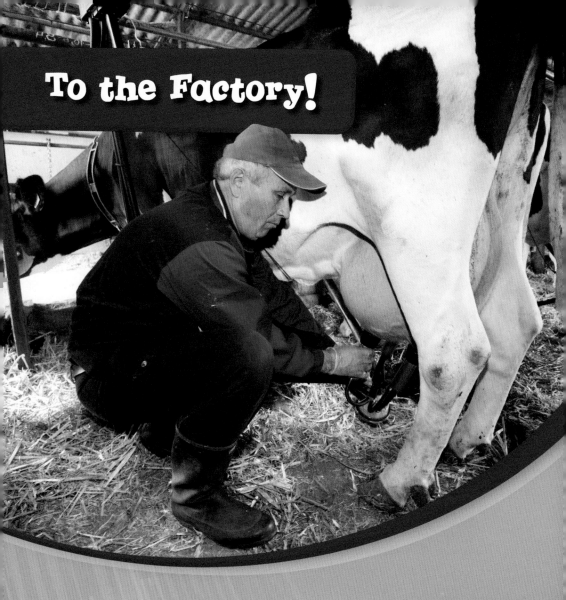

Farmers use machines to milk cows. The fresh milk travels through tubes to **vats**.

Vats store and cool the milk.

Next, the milk goes into milk trucks. The trucks visit dairy farms every day.

milk truck

Truck drivers bring milk to the ice cream factory!

Mixed and Frozen

At the factory, the milk is stored. Then the milk goes into a vat.

It is mixed with cream, sugar, and **stabilizers**. Stabilizers keep the ice cream smooth.

Milk Needed to Make Ice Cream

3 gallons (11 liters) of whole milk are needed to make 1 gallon (4 liters) of ice cream

The ice cream is **pasteurized**. This removes harmful **bacteria**. Then it is **homogenized** to keep the ice cream creamy.

ice cream pasteurizer machine

Next, flavors like chocolate or vanilla are added!

barrel freezer

The flavored ice cream goes into a **barrel freezer**. Inside, a **dasher** mixes air into the ice cream.

Then candy and other toppings can be added.

cartons

The ice cream is poured into cartons. Then it is put into a **blast freezer** to harden.

Once the ice cream is frozen, the cartons are put into boxes.

A freezer truck takes the ice cream to stores. The ice cream is put on shelves. People buy the ice cream to enjoy!

Milk to Ice Cream

1. milk is stored in vats

2. milk is taken to the factory

3. milk is mixed with sugar, cream, and stabilizers

4. ice cream is pasteurized, homogenized, and flavored

5. air is mixed into ice cream as it freezes

6. ice cream is packaged, frozen, and shipped to stores

Ready to Eat!

Many people eat ice cream in bowls, on cones, or on sticks. Others enjoy ice cream sandwiches.

Ice cream is a yummy treat for all ages!

Glossary

bacteria—very tiny living things that can cause someone to get sick

barrel freezer—a round freezer

blast freezer—a freezer that quickly cools and hardens things

dasher—a paddle inside a barrel freezer that mixes air into ice cream

homogenized—to have the fat in milk broken up; homogenizing makes ice cream creamy.

pasteurized—heated and cooled to remove harmful bacteria and keep the milk fresh longer

process—a number of steps taken to reach an end result

stabilizers—substances put in some foods to keep them in a certain condition

vats—large tanks used to store liquids; vats are used on dairy farms to store milk.

To Learn More

AT THE LIBRARY

Bailey, R. J. *Ice Cream: How Is it Made?* Minneapolis, Minn.: Jump!, 2017.

Grack, Rachel. *Grass to Milk*. Minneapolis, Minn.: Bellwether Media, 2020.

Hansen, Grace. *How Is Ice Cream Made?* Minneapolis, Minn.: Abdo Kids, 2018.

ON THE WEB

FACTSURFER

Factsurfer.com gives you a safe, fun way to find more information.

1. Go to www.factsurfer.com.
2. Enter "milk to ice cream" into the search box and click 🔍.
3. Select your book cover to see a list of related content.

Index

air, 14
bacteria, 12
barrel freezer, 14
blast freezer, 16
bowls, 20
cartons, 16, 17
cones, 20
cows, 5, 6
cream, 11
dairy farms, 5, 8
dasher, 14
factory, 9, 10
farmers, 6
flavors, 13, 14
freezer truck, 18
homogenized, 12
materials, 11
milk trucks, 8, 9
milk usage, 12
pasteurized, 12, 13
process, 5

sandwiches, 20
stabilizers, 11
steps, 19
sticks, 20
stores, 18
sugar, 11
toppings, 15
treat, 21
vats, 6, 7, 10
who eats ice cream, 5

The images in this book are reproduced through the courtesy of: P Maxwell Photography, front cover (ice cream); Image Craft, front cover (milk); Anton Starikov, p. 3; Torwaistudio, pp. 4-5; bibiphoto, pp. 6-7; Yuangeng Zhang, pp. 7, 19 (step 1); Photoagriculture, pp. 8-9; Bjoern Wylezich, pp. 9, 19 (step 2); Eric Carr/ Alamy, pp. 10-11, 19 (step 3); Ronaldo Almeida, p. 11 (milk); Elena Gordeichik, p. 11 (cream); Timmary, p. 11 (sugar); baranozdemir, pp. 12-13, 19 (step 4); tenmay, pp. 14-15, 19 (step 5); Nataly Studio, p. 15; Syda Productions, pp. 16-17; Bloomberg / Contributor/ Getty, pp. 17, 19 (step 6); Joni Hanebutt, p. 18; Pikul Noorod, pp. 20-21; AaresTT, p. 21; M. Unal Ozmen, p. 22.

HELEN HALLER
ELEMENTARY LIBRARY
350 Fir Street
Sequim, WA 98382